Roister Doister Publishing

One Act Play

by Matt Fox

About the Author

Matt Fox

Matt Fox started writing for the theatre as a teenager when he joined a writer's group at Plymouth Theatre Royal. Following a degree in English and an MA in Professional Writing he started to write, produce and direct theatrical productions.

Matt's has written plays, operas and musical adaptations which have been performed in the UK, US and Australia. His play *To Sleep* was staged in the West End in September 2013 and toured the UK & Australia in 2014/15. His latest plays *Family Play* and *The Life We Lived* are touring the UK simultaneously in 2016. His best known piece of work is *Swindon: the Opera*, which was written with internationally acclaimed composer Betty Roe MBE, and performed in July 2012.

Matt's work is published by Roister Doister Publishing Ltd and Off The Wall Plays in the UK, and JD Drama Publishing in the USA.

Originally from Cornwall, Matt moved to Swindon in 2006. He is a trustee for music education charity the JTPTrust, writer, producer & co-director of production company Madam Renards Ltd as well as the co-founder of the Swindon Fringe Festival.

One Act Play

by Matt Fox

First published in Great Britain in 2016 by
Roister Doister Publishing
The Swan Theatre
The Moors
Worcester
WR1 3ED
info@roisterdoister.com
www.roisterdoister.com

ISBN: 978-0-9932619-6-1

CHARACTERS

Man
50s/60s

Woman
50s/60s

SETTING
A bedroom. A double bed.

One Act Play was first produced by Madam Renards Theatre Co. on the 6th April 2013 at Steam, Swindon.

CAST

Man   Peter Edge-Partington

Woman   Mary Farragher

PRODUCTION TEAM

Directors   Mary Farragher & Peter Edge Partington

One Act Play

A One Act Play

by Matt Fox

ONE ACT PLAY

The man and woman are in the bed. They are sat up in the bed next to each other.
Both have an individual spotlight, so they can be lit or unlit as required. Both speak in
exaggerated Yorkshire accents. Spotlight comes up on Woman.

Woman
Les Miserables...by heck what a show...by heck...and by gum for that matter as
well. That Jean Val Jean...by gum, by heck...lovely beard...you can always trust
a man with a good beard...not worried about his vibrating razors or his face
ointment. Likes to show off his masculinity...wears it right there on his face
for all to see...lovely man that Jean Val Jean. Apparently Les Miserables means
'The Miserables'...it's a funny old language that French...nothing like English
really...'The Miserables'...lucky they kept with the French really otherwise
nobody would have gone...needs the mystical nature of a foreign language to
really sound like a show worth seeing...no one down our way would go and
see The Miserables...but Les Miserables...well that sounds like culture...I have
to say the other characters in it weren't a patch on old Jean Val Jean though
by gum...Barely a beard between them...you can't wave a revolutionary flag
without a good beard to hang your message of freedom from...that's where
that William Wallace went wrong...probably the reason why the English
executed him if you want my opinion...face like a baby's bum that chap had
by heck and not so much as a flat cap or whippet to bring to the bargain.
Lovely man Jean Val Jean though...shame he weren't from Yorkshire really.

Spot fades on Woman and comes up on Man.

Man
I was down T'park T'other day when I saw T'at William T'Shakspeare was
putting on one of his T'Plays. Two T'Gentlemen of V'T 'rona I believe it
were called. I do love William T'Shakespeare...lovely fella...lovely writer...bit
T'morbid now and then but a lovely writer...liked a whippet I believe...took
'em down T'Globe to seeT'plays...clever fella. Saw T'R, T'S, T'C that's T'R, T'S,
T'Cs production of Anthony and Cleopatra last year...lovely production...no
whippets mind, but lovely none the less...got great reviews from T'Guardian
and T'Newsnight Review...lovely fella that T'Shakespeare.

Spot fades on Man and comes up on Woman.

Woman
Now the Yorkshire dialect's a funny old thing...you'd have to be born and
bred there like me to fully appreciate the subtle nuances of it. Born and bred
with a flat cap and a pint of mild and a job in steelworks. Cos that's what
you do in Yorkshire. Get job in steelworks, wait for steelworks to close down,
stand on dole queue and finally form all male stripper troop to entertain
the Yorkshire wives of the unemployed Yorkshire men. That's the Yorkshire
dream...and grow a beard...that's important too...shows the whippet who's
boss.

Spot fades on Woman and come up on Man.

Man
As I said, I was down T'Park with T'William T'Shakespeare, when I saw T'
Ships come sailing in...

Looks quizzical but starts to speak again.

...T ships come sailing in...wait...it weren't T'Christmas...this is getting T'silly...
and why was T'William T'Shaksepeare standing with me looking at T'Ships?
He's T'dead...has been for fourT'undred years.

Spot comes up on Woman.

Woman
Now this accent has gone far enough...at least three of the those T's had
no right being placed in a sentence like that...there was me explaining the
Yorkshire dialect...as someone who's actually from Yorkshire and there's you
putting T's where they don'T belong.

Man
Well you emphasised the T in that don't far too much...are you trying T make
some sort of clever point?

Woman
There you go again...the word's 'to' not 'T'. You're missing the vowel
alT'gether.

Man
Me? You just...anyway wha'T are you doing T'alking about Jean Val bloody
Jean and Les Miser – bloody – rables. What's that got to do with anything?

Woman
I was merely using him...played by Colm Wilkinson in the original production
I might add...as an example of why Yorkshire men should have beards.

Man
Yorkshire men? Jean Val Jean's supposed to be French...I doubt he'd ever
been to Yorkshire...and Colm Wilkinson was Irish...I think Alfie Boe is from
Yorkshire though.

Woman
Who's Alfie Boe?

Man
You mean you don't know? The one bit of information that would make your
link between Yorkshire and Les Miserables at least vaguely make sense and
you don't know!...Alfie Boe is the current Jean Val Jean in the current London
show...and he's a bloody Yorkshireman!

Woman
And they let him play Jean Val Jean?

Man
Aye...didn't seem to think being from Yorkshire was an impediment.

Woman
By gum.

Man
Aye, by gum.

They sit in silence for a time looking at the audience, sighing and looking around.

Woman
So why all that stuff about Shakespeare? Some sort of attempt to out-culture me in front of people? Shakespeare was as populist as Claude-Michel Schonberg in his time...don't think just cos they study him at universities that he's any more high-brow than anyone else.

Man
What about that Andrew Lloyd Webber?

Woman
Well maybe him...but no one else.

Man
Fair enough.

Woman
You're allowed the occasional T by the way. You seem to have lost them alT'gether now.

Man
Well you made me feel a little self-conscious to tell the truth...I didn't want T'over do it.

Woman
There you go...everything in'T moderation.

There is a pause.

Man
So why exactly are we sat here in bed? It's not like we know each other or anything?

Woman
By heck no...you are certainly not the sort of person that I'd usually find myself in bed with.

Man
Why?

Woman
You're just not...not really something I want to get into with them watching?

Indicates audience.

Man
I'm glad you can see them too...I thought it was just me...was it you that broke it then?

Woman
Broke what?

Man
The fourth wall...it wasn't when you took your shoes off to get into bed was it? You can do a lot of damage with a rough stiletto heel...

Looks out at audience.

Far more damage than I imagine both of us thought.

They both raise a hand and wave nervously at the audience – there is a pause.

Woman
Well I guess there's nothing to do except carry on and hope no-one notices. I'm sure whoever owns it'll be properly insured. You have to be in this day and age.

Man
Oh aye by gum...everyone's been insured since that Brecht started on his escapades.

Woman
Brecht?

Man
Bertolt Brecht, German fella...there was a time when you couldn't do anything without old Brecht breaking a fourth wall...it pushed the premiums right up so it did.

Woman
They never think about the consequences these epic theatre vandals...one minute you're watching a nice play and the next your knee deep in semiotics. Anyone would think that playwrights thought theatre should have an intellectual purpose.

Man
Not me...give me a nice musical comedy with some song and dance numbers any day. That's what the people want...not this pretentious rubbish with placards and direct addresses to the audience.

Woman
Oh aye.

Man
By gum.

There is a pause.

Man
So what do we do with them?

Indicates the audience.

Woman
I'd just ignore them and hope they go away – just get on with our everyday lives.

The Man considers this for a while.

Man
What everyday lives?...I've never met you before and I certainly don't know how we ended up in this bed...to be honest I'm not altogether sure how I ended up with this accent or how I know any of things I just talked about.

Woman
Aye...I say I'm born and bred in Yorkshire, but to be honest I don't even know where Yorkshire is.

Man
Nor me...but now you come to mention it I think Alfie Boe might be from Lancashire anyway...you got any idea what a whippet is by the way?

Woman
Nay by gum.

Man
Well we must have come from somewhere...how did you know about Les Miserables and Jean Val Jean's beard?

Woman
Well I think my character was primed with that knowledge, so they could make that strange opening monologue, inciting laughter and confusion with the audience in equal measure.

Man
I think any laughter came from your obviously fake accent rather than the contents of the script.

Woman
Script? You mean someone wrote what I said?

Man
Well it seems that way...not quite sure why they bothered to be fair...seems like drivel to me.

Woman
Aye you're right there.

Man
But how did they manage to implant the words in our heads?

Woman
And who are they?

Both look around the room.

Woman
Do you think they're here right now?

Man
Could be...to be honest apart from the bed, I'm not sure where the rest of this room is?

Woman
They could be out there?

Indicates the audience.

Woman
Hidden amongst the crowds.

They both lean forward looking at the audience.

Man
Aye...bastard.

Woman
Bloody bastard.

They both sit in the bed looking uncomfortable, fiddling with the bed sheets etc.

Man
We could just leave.

Woman
Aye we could...where to though?

Man
Well this building must be situated somewhere? We could leave now and start a life somewhere.

Woman
Me and you?

Man
Why not? Do you know anyone else?

Woman
Well no...can't say I do...you?

Man
Never met anyone else in me life...not sure how I even have language if I'm being fully honest...no one taught me.

Woman
It's from him.

Points into the audience.

Man
Him?

Woman
The writer.

Man
How do you know it's an him? There's all sorts out there.

Woman
Only a 'him' would be so cruel.

Man
That's a pretty firm view on the nature of masculinity for someone who's never been anywhere or met anyone or done anything.

Woman
I've met you.

Man
Aye...and I've met you. But how do we know we're male or female? Is that from 'him' as well?

Woman
Aye.

Man
Well I think I'm probably a man – not that I'm overly sure what a man is.

Woman
But what about your last statement on the nature of masculinity? You seem to know that a man is masculine.

Man
Aye, but what's masculine?

Woman
I have a feeling that that's a question that even people who have been conscious of their world for more than ten flippin' minutes wouldn't fully know.

Man
Why's that?

Woman
Because it sounds like the sort of question that maybe people would debate endlessly, going round and round in circles, until they finally admit that they haven't a clue.

Man
Oh aye, and what about femininity?

Woman
What's that?

Man
Well I think...and again I don't know where this is coming from...but I think femininity is like the woman version of masculinity.

Woman
But what's the difference?

Man
I don't rightly know.

Woman
Well what's the difference between me and you?

Man
Mm.

Surveys himself and then her.

Man
You've got smaller hands than me.

Woman
Aye...and you've got a bigger jaw.

Man
Aye.

Woman
You've got a deeper voice than me.

Man
True...and you've got tits.

Woman
So've you.

Man
Aye.

Woman
Well if that's it then I don't know whether there's much to debate.

Man
Aye no.

They both sit and reflect for a moment.

Man
So why did you say only a man could be so cruel?

Woman
I don't know...seemed like the sort of thing a person would say...don't know why though...are you cruel?

Man
I'm not too sure what cruel is, but I'm inclined to say no...I think I'm pretty uncruel.

Woman
Uncruel? Is that a word? Seems difficult to define being uncruel if you don't know what being cruel is?

Man
Something about putting cats in bins rings a bell? Not that I'm overly sure what a cat or a bin is?

Woman
Or whether you could put a bin in a cat?

Man
I think that's probably even crueller truth be told.

Woman
Aye...I think you're probably right.

Pause.

Man
So what about this idea of getting away?

Woman
What about it?

Man
Well do you think we could?

Woman
I guess so. Like we said though...we don't know where the writer is or what he's planned for us. We might be part of an intricate narrative structure, and these apparently random utterances could be leading to a cleverly crafted finale where the true meaning of the piece is revealed for all to see.

Man
I doubt it...I have a feeling that he actually just started writing and hoped that he'd end up with enough to fulfil the minimum duration requirements.

Woman
Minimum duration requirements for what?

Man
Some sort of...I don't know...festival of theatre...where...let me think...someone would be judging the artistic merits of a production in front of a crowd of theatrical intellectuals.

Woman
Theatrical intellectuals? By heck...I doubt that very much...I imagine it'll be in front of a room full of inebriated half wits who've entered the place by mistake in an attempt to find the nearest toilet...I'd be surprised if the room wasn't already stinking of stale urine and BO.

Man
Aye you're probably right.

Pauses.

Woman
But on the up side, that should make escape a little more straightforward... theatrical intellectuals would know if the characters on stage just got up and left...the audience the writer will have, wouldn't notice if a tectonic fault line opened up in the earth and the stage disappeared into the white hot magma below.

Man
No...I don't suppose they would.

Woman
So how will we do it then?

Man
Well I believe the usual method is to get out of bed, stand up and run towards the exit.

Woman
Aye...that's probably the best plan.

Man
The only problem is whether the willing suspension of disbelief will cover us, until we're safely away.

Woman
Well how big is it?

Man
Again...that really depends who's in. For some it'll be broken the moment we go past the proscenium arch...for others we could probably take up residence in their spare bedroom and they'd still think the play was going on.

Woman
Those ones must be the greatest artistic minds of them all.

Man
Or the most pretentious.

Woman
It's a difficult thing to judge.

Man
I think the trick will be, to make them think that it's somehow part of the action – something the writer had planned.

Woman
But I think we've established that they'll be pretty sure by this point that he's planned nothing.

Man
Aye...it's a risk.

Woman
Maybe the writer will help us?

Man
Why on earth would he do that? He hasn't bothered explaining who we are, why we're here, why I apparently knew who Shakespeare was, why you seem to be a fan of through-composed musicals people like to cry along to, or indeed...what the bloody point of all these people forking out their hard earned cash to see an endless barrage of ego boosting, self aggrandising, pseudo-intellectual bollocks played out without any apparent purpose or endpoint in site. As far as I can see, and to be fair I've only been exposed to him as an abstract concept, he appears to be a grade-A twat with no interest in anything except his own self worth.

Woman
He seems to have stimulated an anger-like emotion in you...almost like he's created you and then selfishly left you to your own devices without so much as a sign or word to confirm his existence.

Man
Oh you're getting a little deep there...I'd just stick with the musicals...We don't want to start questioning our own existence after all...we don't know where that'll lead.

Woman
Aye...you're right...let's just believe in the writer, even though he's a twat, and get on with our escape plan.

Man
Aye that's the spirit...so a plan of escape.

Woman
We've covered get up and run...what next?

Man
Well as we don't know what's out there, I think we're gonna have to play most of it by ear?

Woman
What does that mean?

Man
It's a saying...I don't know what it actually means, but I think it suggests that we need to take things as they come.

Woman
Which means what?

Man
You know...wing it?

Woman looks quizzical.

Man
Ad-lib?

Woman still looks quizzical.

Man
Go off the cuff?

Woman still looks quizzical.

Man
Well anyway – I don't think anyone's gonna help us and we don't know what to expect, so its just you and me against the world now, look up there in the sky now, there's a star that's shining just for us.

Woman
But we're inside.

Man
Shut up.

Woman
OK...so what shall we aim to do once we've played it by ear, taken things as they come, winged it and ad-libbed?

Man
Not forgetting gone off the cuff...we could stop somewhere...we could do something...we could belong to some place.

Woman
You could almost say that there's a place for us, somewhere a place for us...if you hold my hand, we're halfway there...a place for us somewhere.

Man
Now you're getting it.

Woman
So what would we live in?

Man
Live in?

Woman
Well I believe that when people go somewhere and end up somewhere, they tend to stay in some kind of building. A house or a flat.

Man
A caravan even?

Woman
Aye, even a caravan...as long as it's somewhere to call their own.

Man
And you're sure if we live in a caravan people won't start to make preconceptions about us and get some sort of mass audience broadcasting system to view us from a biased point of view, so that those who conform to a more mainstream cultural normality can sit in their brick built houses and flats and laugh at why we're different to them?

Woman
No...I don't think that would happen...it's not like everyone's an arrogant twat like the writer.

Man
Praise be.

Woman
What?

Man
Well it's probably best to at least pretend to be thankful to him? You never know when he could be watching.

Woman
But five minutes ago you were saying how much of a pretentious idiot he was.

Man
Aye...but he's the only one we've got and we should at least give the impression of being faithful.

Woman
Faithful?

Man
Aye...he might get angry and take vengeance out upon us.

Woman
Well we've been slagging him off for the past quarter of an hour and he's not done anything yet...I'm gonna take a punt on this and suggest that he isn't listening at all.

Man
OK...well at least keep your voice down and pretend to be obedient...if you are indeed a woman, I believe they have a pretty poor record when it comes to doing what their creators tell them.

Woman
And where are you getting that from? We've existed less than an hour.

Man
Just a gut feeling...

Woman
Well don't tell anyone else or they'll start to think it's true.

Man
Fair enough...so what about this place to live then?

Woman
Well I've always imagined a place with green fields and trees, where you can hear the sound of wild birds in the morning and the gentle bubbling of a brook as you lay your head on your pillow at the end of the day...and before you say it, I know that I don't know what trees, fields and birds are or whether brooks bubble or not...and I'm fully aware that I can't have always imagined anything because it seems I've never existed until this moment...but.

Man
But.

Woman
That's still what I want, and in the absence of anything else to define me and give me a sense of who I am and what I'm about, I'm gonna hang onto it and let the world know that that is my humble dream.

Man
Aye...well good for you...I'm afraid I don't know what I want or don't want... I'm no dreamer like you...all I'm interested in is getting away from here and trying my hand at a life...any life'll do, as long as it's on my terms and you're with me.

Woman
You know, for something that started out fairly cold and abstract, this is all turning a little musical theatre for my liking.

Man
*(Regretfully)*Aye.

Woman
So what about after we've escaped, set up a house...

Man
Or caravan

Woman
...Or caravan...what then?

Man
We could procreate.

Woman
Well as we've established that we're really none the wiser about the difference between a man and a woman, I'm not overly sure whether we're qualified to try something like that. To be honest I'm not sure how you even go about it?

Man
Nor am I to be fair, I imagine it's one of those things that becomes fairly clear when the time is right...for all we know we could be procreating right now.

Woman
I'd imagine that I'd be more aware of what was going on?

Man
Not necessarily...I've a feeling that in some cases, where for example a person had consumed a great deal of some kind of inebriating, mind numbing, sleep inducing elixir, you could probably procreate without even realising you'd done so... which could cause some issues I'd wager.

Woman
Aye...well assuming we're not procreating right now, but we do work out how to procreate at some point, what would we do with the procreatee?

Man
Look I'm almost certain that procreatee isn't a word...I don't think that you can just create nouns from vowels like that...I imagine that people have written endless books ont' subject, and there are whole societies based on the defence of proper language.

Woman
But surely language would be something that evolved and developed like a living species...not something that you can box up and shackle.

Man
Evolved like a species...what are you saying...surely all life were created by the writer like us?

Woman
Aye...it would be easy to think that...but there's a part of me that thinks that no- one's in charge of what's going on right now. Like it's all a load of random occurrences which have accidentally created the world that we can now see.

Man
What...no writer?

Woman
Aye... why not?

Man
Oh I don't know about that...sounds like dangerous thinking to me...I know we've established that he's not exactly at the top of his game on this one, and that he was probably rushing it...but if there's no writer then what is there?

Woman
I don't know...but isn't that exciting, not to know?

Man
Do you think they know?

Indicates the audience.

Woman
I doubt it...some might think they do, but I don't think so.

Man
By gum...this is scary stuff.

Woman
So it is by heck.

Man
Well at least we've got some by gums and by hecks back...I was starting to wonder where they'd gone...

Pause.

Man
So what would happen to this product of procreation...what would we tell them?

Woman
I don't know...maybe we'd let them work stuff out for themselves.

Man
Aye...well we seem to have worked out a lot in the last half an hour...imagine what they could work out in a full lifetime.

Woman
Aye by heck.

They sit and reflect for a moment.

Man
(Whispers to the Woman whilst indicating the audience) I haven't heard them laugh for a while.

Woman
(Whispers back) That's 'cos I don't think we've been very funny for a good while.

Man
You know if there is a writer, he could have staged all of this to make some sort of point about something or other. He could be playing an elaborate game of cat and mouse with us...

Woman
Nah...no one could have written such a rambling pile of nonsense...if anything the lack of structure, laughs, purpose or indeed basic writing skill has proved that the writer does not exist, and I'm prepared to fully state now and in front of everyone...

Man
Including them?

Indicates the audience.

Woman
Aye...including them...sat there looking at us through that broken fourth wall, with Bertolt Brecht holding up a placard saying this is a play and Stanislavsky was a bell-end...in front of all of that, I'm going to place my cards on the table.

Man goes to say something.

I know I don't have any cards or a table and no concept of what they are, but that all said, I'm prepared to state that I am an a-writerist.

Man
Is that even a word?

Woman
Well I imagine it would be more eloquently expressed if you were to use ancient Greek, but as I've only been alive for thirty minutes, I think I'm at liberty to coin a new word for the purpose.

Man
Aye...I guess you would be...so what do we do now?

Woman
We escape...we renounce the mind-forged manacles of the writer and we leave as masters of our own destiny.

Man
I'm not sure about this...what if the writer is real?

Woman
And what if he isn't...do you want to live your life wondering what if...
imagining what could have been?

Man
I guess not.

Woman
Then let's go.

Man
OK...let's go.

The Man and Woman pause for a moment in anticipation of what they are about to do, then slowly they turn around as if to jump out of bed. They lurch but then stop, they lurch again, but do not leave the bed.

Man
What's wrong?

Woman
I don't know...it's like I can't move.

Man
Aye...like we're rooted to the spot.

They look at each other and after a moment reach under the covers to where their legs appear to be.

Woman
Oh no.

Man
Aye...Oh no.

They take hold of their 'legs' and pull them above the covers, revealing them to be nothing but pillows arranged as legs; slowly they pull away the covers altogether to reveal a fake bed made of hardboard, printed with markings that show it's scenery. They then look down at their bodies and see that their nightdress/nightshirts are stapled to the hardboard, the upper halves of their bodies being all that they have. They both look down for a moment and then finally look back up.

Man
I guess the top half's all he needed for this play.

Woman
Why waste money on legs when a few pillows would create the illusion.

Man
So is this it then?

Woman
Looks like it, aye.

Man
By gum.

Woman
Aye...by heck.

They both pause for a moment.

Man
Would have been nice through...to get away.

Woman
Aye...would of...would of have been grand so it would.

Man
So is that the end then?

Woman
Well that was the final piece of exposition...the twist if you like...that's the final thing that was left to say.

Man
And he knew that from the start...sat out there... *(Points to the audience)* ...pretending he's smart...telling himself that there's no place for pathos in an abstract piece of experimentalism.

Woman
Aye...bastard.

Man
Bastard.

They both sit there looking forward.

Woman
Well it was fun whilst it lasted I guess...

Man
Aye...by gum it was.

Woman
Night love.

Man
Aye...Night.

They move in and give each other a delicate kiss on the lips.

Blackout.

End

Roister Doister Publishing

Founded in 2013 Roister Doister Publishing was created to rethink theatrical publishing, give a quality start to new writers and a more 'in touch' approach to established writers. Roister Doister Publishing endeavours to make writing, publishing, and producing theatre as easy as possible for both professionals and amateurs.

HOW DOES ROISTER DOISTER PUBLISHING DIFFER FROM OTHER PUBLISHERS?

Upfront and Up-to-date Information

All the information you need to make a decision regarding a play will be at your disposal from the moment you look at our website. License fees, availability, and permissions will all be on the play's Roister Doister page enabling you to make the right decision for your company.

Quality Control

Unlike other online 'publishers' we will not just blindly accept any script for 'publication'. We will give each script submitted to us careful consideration and advice before we release it to the public, even in our New Work section.

Investment in our Playwrights

All great theatre begins with a great play. We will invest in our writer's work and creative property by not only providing a store front for their scripts but also a professional profile for the writer where they can build their public awareness.

If you enjoyed this script please ask your local library to stock our titles.